Chicago Bee Branch
3647 S. State Street
Chicago, IL 60609

A Kid's Guide
to the
Classification
of
Living Things ™

Plants
With
Seeds

Elaine Pascoe

Photographs by Dwight Kuhn

The Rosen Publishing Group's
PowerKids Press ™
New York

Published in 2003 by The Rosen Publishing Group, Inc.
29 East 21st Street, New York, NY 10010

First Edition

Editor: Natashya Wilson
Book Design: Emily Muschinske
Layout: Eric DePalo

Photo Credits: All photos © Dwight Kuhn.

Pascoe, Elaine.
Plants with seeds / Elaine Pascoe; photography by Dwight Kuhn.— 1st ed.
    p. cm. — (A kid's guide to the classification of living things)
Summary: Details the life cycles and characteristics of plants that use seeds to reproduce.
Includes bibliographical references (p.   ).
  ISBN 0-8239-6314-4 (lib. bdg.)
1. Plants—Juvenile literature. 2. Phanerogams—Juvenile literature. [1. Plants. 2. Seeds.] I. Kuhn, Dwight, ill.
II. Title.
  QK49 .P18 2003
  580—dc21
                                                                    2001007793

Manufactured in the United States of America

Contents

Classifying Living Things

How is a daisy like a pine tree? How is it different? By asking questions like these, scientists organize living things in nature to understand them better. Scientists sort living things into groups based on the ways that they are alike.

Sorting things this way is called classification. You can find examples of classification everywhere. In a toy store, action figures are in one section. Video games are in another section, and dolls are in a third section. The toys are placed with other toys like them.

Scientists usually sort living things into five **kingdoms**. Each kingdom is then sorted into smaller groups, as the diagram shows. This book is about one group in the plant kingdom, plants with seeds.

Scientists sort living things into the five kingdoms on the top row first. Here the plant kingdom is sorted into smaller and smaller groups.

  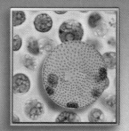  

Fungus Kingdom **Animal Kingdom** **Plant Kingdom** **Protist Kingdom** **Monera Kingdom**

Plants With Seeds **Plants Without Seeds**

Gymnosperms **Angiosperms**

White Pine **White Spruce** **Shasta Daisies** **Sugar Maple**

The Plant Kingdom

All plants are alike in some ways. Unlike animals, plants grow in fixed places. They make their own food inside their leaves. Leaves contain materials called **pigments** that capture the energy in sunlight. The leaves use this energy to turn water and **carbon dioxide**, a gas in the air, into a kind of sugar that feeds the plant. This process is called **photosynthesis**. Pigments also give leaves their colors. The most common pigment, **chlorophyll**, is green.

Some plants make seeds. Some do not. Plants that make seeds are **complex** plants. They have roots that grow down into the ground. The roots soak up water and other **nutrients**. These nutrients travel up the plant stem to the leaves, helping the plant to grow.

Nutrients travel from the roots of this red maple tree, a complex plant, up through its trunk, branches, and leaves.

Seeds

Seeds are one way by which plants **reproduce**. Each seed has everything needed to start a new plant. Inside the hard outer coating of a seed is a tiny new plant. The seed also holds a supply of stored food for the new plant.

Plants spread seeds in many ways. Wind, water, or passing animals help to spread the seeds. If a seed lands in a place with good soil and water, it **sprouts**. A root pushes out of the seed into the soil. A stem grows up toward the light, and **seed leaves** open.

Some plants' seeds are carried inside fruit. These plants are called flowering plants, or **angiosperms**. Other plants do not make fruit. These plants are called **gymnosperms**. Gymnosperm means "naked seed."

This sunflower seed has started to sprout. Sunflowers are angiosperms. Their seeds are carried inside striped shells.

Conifers: Pines and More

Conifers are the largest group of gymnosperms. You can tell a conifer by the cones that grow on its branches. These cones hold a conifer's seeds. Pine, fir, spruce, cedar, and hemlock trees are conifers. So are giant sequoia trees, some of the biggest living things on Earth. They can grow up to 328 feet (100 m) tall and can weigh more than 2,000 tons (1,814 t). Some conifers grow to be only a few inches (cm) tall.

Most conifers have woody stems called trunks. Their leaves are shaped like needles or scales. A leaf stays green until it is ready to be shed. Then it turns brown and falls off. Unlike many trees, conifers do not lose all their leaves in the fall. They shed old leaves throughout the year, so conifers look green all year long.

Conifers grow in almost every part of the world, but many kinds grow best in cool places. This white pine tree is growing in Maine.

These young plants are the beginnings of sunflowers. The seeds have sprouted. Roots are growing down into the ground. Stems are growing up toward the light. The seed leaves are opening.

This small plant is the beginning of an oak tree. Under the ground its roots are soaking in water and nutrients. This will help the young tree to grow. The thin stem will thicken into a big trunk, and the tree will grow many leaves and branches.

You may not think of maple trees as flowering plants, but they are! Here a Norway maple shows its flowers. Maple trees are angiosperms.

Cones such as these are a sure sign that a plant is a conifer. The pointy, needlelike leaves are also found on most conifers. This conifer is a white spruce tree.

Conifers: Cones and Seeds

Conifers have two kinds of cones, male and female. The female cones are usually made up of woody scales. They produce **egg cells**. The male cones are quite small. They produce **pollen**, a grainy powder that will **fertilize** the egg cells. In the spring, the male cones open and release clouds of pollen. Some of the pollen lands on the female cones. The male and female cells join, and seeds begin to form.

When the seeds are ready, the cone's scales spread open to let them go. The seeds of pines and many other conifers have little wings. The wind catches the wings and carries the seeds away. New conifers may grow wherever they land.

The pink-tipped female cones on this tamarack tree make seeds. The tan-colored male cone makes pollen.

Conifers are gymnosperms, so their seeds do not have outer coatings. This is the inside of a white pine's cone. The oval-shaped seeds can be seen at the bottom of the picture.

This is the female cone of a white pine tree. A white pine's leaves, or needles, grow to be from 2 to 4 inches (5–10 cm) long. The needles grow in bunches of five.

These white-pine cones have opened to let out their seeds. The seeds may land beneath the tree, or may be carried farther away by the wind. The seeds may also be eaten or moved by animals.

Many Kinds of Flowering Plants

The angiosperm group is made up of the flowering plants. They include garden plants, oak trees, and grasses. Flowering plants have flat leaves. They carry their seeds inside fruit. Angiosperm means "vessel seed." The fruit is a vessel, or container, for the seeds.

Scientists sort flowering plants into two groups called **monocots** and **dicots**. Grasses, corn, and wheat are monocots. Their leaves have veins in rows, like stripes. The tiny new plants inside their seeds have just one seed leaf.

Most trees and many common flowers and vegetables are dicots. The veins in their leaves form branching networks. Their new plants have two seed leaves.

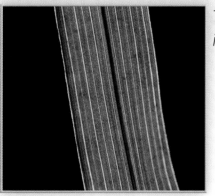

The veins in the leaf of a monocot run in straight lines, as shown here.

These are corn seeds. Corn is a monocot.

The veins in the leaf of a dicot have many branches, as shown here.

Daisies are dicots. When new daisies first sprout, they have two seed leaves.

Flowers

Flowers are seed factories. Some flowering plants have separate male and female flowers. However, in most flowering plants, the male and female parts are in the middle of the same flower. The male parts are called **stamens**. They are long stalks that make pollen. The female parts are called **pistils**. The base of a pistil holds egg cells. The pistil also has a sticky tip that can catch pollen.

Pollen reaches a pistil in a number of ways. Wind may carry it. Insects spread pollen, too. Bees and other insects feed on **nectar**, a sugary liquid that flowers make. The insects brush against the stamens and are dusted with pollen. As they feed, they spread pollen from flower to flower.

The stalk in the center of this lily is the pistil, the flower's female part. It is surrounded by the pollen-covered stamens, the male parts.

Grasses, including lawn grass, are monocots. Lawn grass doesn't usually get a chance to flower, because it is always being mowed.

Before they can grow fruit, apple trees must blossom with flowers. Apple trees are dicots.

Flowers' bright colors help them to attract bees and other insects that help to pollinate the flowers.

The stamens of this lily have dark tops. The pistil is the thicker green stalk in the middle of the flower.

When this string bean seed is cut in two, you can see the tiny new plant that is inside, ready to grow.

Bumblebees carry pollen from stamens to pistils as they collect nectar from flowers.

Corn leaves show the straight veins of monocots. Corn seeds, called kernels, grow in rows on a cob.

Flowering Plants: Seeds and Fruits

After pollen reaches the pistil, the male and female cells join. Seeds begin to form in the base of the pistil. The flower petals die and fall off, and the base of the pistil swells. It forms the plant's fruit. The fruit protects the seeds. Apples are the fruit made by the flowers of apple trees. An apple has skin and a thick layer of flesh. Inside is a hard case called the core. Inside the core are the seeds.

Apples, peaches, and berries are some fruits that people eat. Vegetables such as beans and pumpkins are fruits, too. Acorns, walnuts, and other nuts are also fruits. The fruits of maple trees look like little nuts with papery wings. The wings catch the wind so that the seeds can spread.

As seeds form in the swollen base of this daffodil's pistil, the flower petals dry up and die. Inset: These are the seeds inside the pistil base.

Flowering Plants: Fall Changes

Some flowering plants die after they produce their seeds. In places where winters are cold, this happens in fall. The seeds of the plants lie on the ground all winter. They sprout in spring.

Other flowering plants shed their leaves each fall and grow new leaves in spring. The leaves of maples and many other trees change color before they drop off, turning orange, yellow, and red. The pigments that make these colors were in the leaves all summer, but the green pigment, chlorophyll, masked them. The chlorophyll breaks down and disappears from the leaves in fall, letting the other colors shine through.

 As the green chlorophyll disappears from the leaves, yellow, orange, and red colors show through.

Peas are the seeds of pea plants. Pea pods are the fruit.

Apple seeds are carried inside the apple fruit. By the time apples grow, the apple blossoms have lost all of their petals.

A sugar maple's seeds have papery, winglike structures that help the wind to carry them away.

These acorns are the fruit of an oak tree. Oak trees are dicots.

In the autumn, the leaves of many angiosperm trees change color and fall off. The trees will grow new leaves in spring.

What Living Things Share

How is a pine tree like a person? The two are more alike than you might think. They are living things.

Living things all reproduce and grow. Trees grow new branches. Children grow taller each year. Living things need food. Plants can make their own food. People and other animals get their food in many ways. Living things can sense the world around them, and they react to what they sense. A sunflower senses sunlight and turns toward the light.

A car does not grow. A television does not sense the world around it. A chair does not eat. These features make nonliving things different from plants and all other living things.

 Rocks are nonliving things. They do not eat, move on their own, or grow.

Glossary

angiosperms (AN-jee-oh-spermz) Plants that have seeds inside fruit.

carbon dioxide (KAR-bin dy-OK-syd) A gas that plants take in from the air and use to make food.

chlorophyll (KLOR-uh-fil) A green coloring in leaves that allows plants to use energy from sunlight to make food.

complex (kahm-PLEKS) Made of many parts.

conifers (KAH-nih-furz) Trees that have needlelike leaves and grow cones.

dicots (DY-kahtz) Plants that have two seed leaves in their seeds.

egg cells (EHG SELZ) Cells made by the female and used to make new life.

fertilize (FER-tih-lyz) To make ready to become a new living thing.

gymnosperms (JIM-noh-spermz) Plants that have seeds without fruit.

kingdoms (KING-duhmz) The five major groups of living things.

monocots (MAH-nuh-kahtz) Plants that have one seed leaf in their seeds.

nectar (NEK-tuhr) A sugary liquid in the center of a flower.

nutrients (NOO-tree-ints) Anything that a living thing needs to live and to grow.

photosynthesis (foh-toh-SYN-thuh-sis) Changing the energy from sunlight into food.

pigments (PIG-mehntz) Materials that give color and have a variety of roles inside cells.

pistils (PIS-tuhlz) The female parts of a flower that develop into fruit.

pollen (PAH-lin) A powder that comes from the male part of a flower.

reproduce (ree-pruh-DOOS) To make babies, to make more of something.

seed leaves (SEED LEEVZ) The leaves of a new plant that form inside the seed and provide food for the plant when it first begins to grow.

sprouts (SPROWT) Begins to grow.

stamens (STAY-muhnz) The male part of a flower, which carries pollen.

Index

Web Sites

Due to the changing nature of Internet links, PowerKids Press has developed an online list of Web sites related to the subject of this book. This site is updated regularly. Please use this link to access the list:
www.powerkidslinks.com/kgclt/plwseed/